I'm Mabel.

THIS BOOK is about women's struggle to win the vote in the 19th and 20th centuries – a struggle which has now succeeded in most countries, but not all. But this is only one part of the story of the right to vote. When the American suffragists and the British suffragettes began their struggle, it wasn't just women who weren't allowed to vote...

In the past, many countries in Africa and Asia were ruled by European colonists, and native people were not allowed to vote. In South Africa, non-white citizens did not have the vote until 1994.

In the United States before 1865, many people of African origin were slaves and had few rights of any kind. Slavery was abolished in 1865, and African-American men were given the right to vote in 1870 – though in reality they were often prevented from voting until the 1960s.

I'm Edith.

IN MANY COUNTRIES, only landowners, or people with a certain amount of money, were allowed to vote. In the United Kingdom this rule was finally abolished in 1928.

In some countries only members of the official religion were allowed to vote. In the United Kingdom, Roman Catholics were refused the vote until 1788.

And yet other people had more than one vote! Graduates of British universities could vote twice: once in their university, and once in the place where they lived. This system was ended in 1948.

Author:
Fiona Macdonald studied history at Cambridge University, England, and at the University of East Anglia. She has taught in schools, adult education and universities, and is the author of numerous books for children on historical topics.

Artist:
David Antram was born in Brighton, England, in 1958. He studied at Eastbourne College of Art and then worked in advertising for fifteen years before becoming a full-time artist. He has illustrated many children's non-fiction books.

Series creator:
David Salariya was born in Dundee, Scotland. He has illustrated a wide range of books and has created and designed many new series for publishers in the UK and overseas. He established The Salariya Book Company in 1989. He lives in Brighton with his wife, illustrator Shirley Willis, and their son Jonathan.

Editors: **Tanya Kant, Stephen Haynes**

Editorial Assistant: **Mark Williams**

Published in Great Britain in 2008 by
Book House, an imprint of
The Salariya Book Company Ltd
25 Marlborough Place, Brighton BN1 1UB
www.salariya.com
www.book-house.co.uk

HB ISBN-13: 978-1-906370-23-7
PB ISBN-13: 978-1-906370-24-4

S A L A R I Y A

1 3 5 7 9 8 6 4 2

A CIP catalogue record for this book is available
from the British Library.

PAPER FROM
SUSTAINABLE
FORESTS

Printed and bound in China.
Printed on paper from sustainable sources.

Avoid Being a
Suffragette!

Written by
Fiona Macdonald

Illustrated by
David Antram

Created and designed by
David Salariya

The Danger Zone

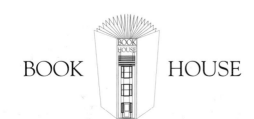

BOOK HOUSE

Not equal!

Great-Aunt Edith begins her story.

'**M**en have been able to vote since Ancient Greek times,* but we women have been banned. Why? Because men would not let us! They claimed that women were weak, stupid and silly! But women have been demanding equality – and the right to vote – for over a hundred years. One of the first was English writer Mary Wollstonecraft. In 1792, her book, *A Vindication of the Rights of Woman*, called for women to be seen as men's partners, not their slaves. I think she was right; don't you?'

* but only if they were free citizens – slaves and foreigners couldn't vote.

FREE SPIRIT. As a lone parent, Mary worked hard to support herself and her young daughter. She wrote books and newspaper articles, ran a home, and helped her many friends. She was a bold, original thinker, who dared to question the way society was organised. For all of her short life (1759–1797) she tried to be independent and free from men's control.

Rights? What rights?

'In the States, too, we've had to fight for our rights. It began in the 1840s. Women campaigning to end slavery also began to demand fair treatment for themselves. They wanted everyone, black or white, male or female, to be equal and free.

'Most women in America had no right to vote, take part in government, own property or have a good education. So, in 1848, Lucretia Mott and Elizabeth Cady Stanton organised the first-ever Women's Convention at Seneca Falls, New York State – to demand equality.'

Edith's American cousin Mabel takes up the story.

Seneca Falls, 1848

MANY SKILLED WOMEN joined the campaign. Elizabeth Cady Stanton was a great writer and researcher. Susan B. Anthony was a rousing speaker. Lucy Stone published a women's rights newspaper. Lucretia Mott was a Quaker minister. Julia Ward Howe wrote poems, including the patriotic 'Battle Hymn of the Republic'.

Elizabeth Cady Stanton 1815–1902

Lucy Stone 1818–1893

Susan B. Anthony 1820–1906

Lucretia Mott 1793–1880

Julia Ward Howe 1819–1910

Even the clothes on your back belong to your husband! In some states, even your children!

Shame!

Shocking!

Handy hint

Keep your own name. Women's rights campaigner Lucy Stone married in 1855 but wouldn't change her name, as a sign of equality. Many men were outraged!

Equal rights? That gets my vote!

SUPPORT FROM FREED SLAVES. Anti-slavery campaigner Frederick Douglass came to the 1848 convention to support women's calls for equality. In 1851, preacher Sojourner Truth proudly claimed that women were as strong and reliable as men: 'Look at me! Look at my arm! I have ploughed and planted, and gathered into barns, and no man could head [do better than] me!'

Sojourner Truth 1797–1883

AT SENECA FALLS, 68 women and 32 men signed the Declaration of Sentiments. It proclaimed: 'All men and women are created equal,' and demanded new laws that would treat American women the same as men.

Frederick Douglass 1818–1895

9

Get noticed!

'The Seneca Falls Convention certainly did inspire women to win the vote. Campaigning was tough and exhausting, but the suffragists' vision of a better, more equal future drove them on. There were many ways to help the cause. Women who stayed at home, looking after their families, raised funds to support their more active sisters. Others travelled across the United States, making speeches, holding meetings and recruiting new supporters.'

SUSAN B. ANTHONY (right) was born to a Quaker family who believed in educating girls. She became a teacher and used her free time to fight against slavery. She decided not to marry, because she wanted independence and freedom to campaign. She travelled all over the United States, making stirring speeches and organising demonstrations. She wrote letters to many powerful men, demanding women's right to vote.

ELIZABETH CADY (left) was very clever but she could not go to university because she was female. She married anti-slavery campaigner Henry Stanton. As well as looking after their seven children, she found time to write books and to compose speeches for her friend Susan B. Anthony. Together they campaigned for women's rights for over 50 years.

This speech will knock their socks off!

10

BE DISRUPTIVE!
In 1876, protesters at the United States Centennial (hundredth anniversary) celebrations in Philadelphia interrupted official speeches and presented a Declaration of Rights for Women to the Vice-President of the United States.

11

Get organised! Advertise!

 'If you were a campaigner in the United States or Britain, how could you win more support for your cause? We'll tell you what those determined 19th-century women did. On both sides of the Atlantic, they took the same decisions – to get organised, and to advertise! They formed committees. They collected signatures for petitions. They lobbied politicians. They put up posters and handed out badges. They set up groups in factories, churches and anywhere else that women met together.'

NOTHING LESS WILL DO!
In 1870, following the abolition of slavery, the US gave the vote to black men. Suffragists were furious that women hadn't been given the same rights. They demanded 'their rights and nothing less!'

In the UK:

1840s: Protesters called Chartists march to demand equal rights and the vote.
1867: The Women's Suffrage Committee in Manchester starts a monster petition.
1897: Local committees link together in a National Union of Women's Suffrage Societies. Now we're getting powerful!

In the US:

1861–1865: Women stop campaigning to nurse injured troops during the Civil War. They win gratitude, but not the vote.
1869: The American Woman Suffrage Association is set up to campaign state by state. The National Woman Suffrage Association aims to change the US Constitution.
1890: The two groups join to form the National American Woman Suffrage Association.

AWSA

NWSA

Did you call us the WEAKER sex?

Slowly, step by step, we'll succeed!

We demand votes – NOW!

DRINK? NO! VOTES? YES! In 1874, the Women's Christian Temperance Union was set up in the US to protest against alcohol abuse. Women now believed that they could change and improve society – all the more reason for them to have the vote.

Beware the demon drink!

'Votes for Women' badge

VOTES FOR WOMEN

Handy hint
Set up a club to discuss new ideas like the vote. The first women's club was founded in the US in 1868. Soon there were hundreds.

Metal badge with portrait of campaign heroine Susan B. Anthony

Yellow roses (and sunflowers) were campaign symbols.

GOLD OR YELLOW was the chosen colour worn by US campaigners. Their British sisters favoured purple, white and green.

VOTES FOR WOMEN

13

Deeds, not words!

Chaining themselves to park railings

'**D**espite all this hard work, by 1900 British women still didn't have the vote. Some were becoming desperate. "How much has 50 years of campaigning achieved? We want results now! And we'll break the law if that's what it takes!"

'In Britain the suffragettes were led by Mrs Emmeline Pankhurst, the widow of a lawyer who had supported equal rights. In 1903 she founded a radical new organisation: the Women's Social and Political Union. It planned to take direct action to win votes for women. Its slogan was: "Deeds, not words!" And some of the actions they took were pretty extreme, I can tell you...'

Breaking shop windows

Setting fire to post boxes

Powerful, passionate Pankhursts

Emmeline Pankhurst was a brave, inspiring leader who attracted many followers – nicknamed 'suffragettes'. Her husband Richard was a campaigning lawyer, and her two daughters, Christabel and Sylvia, were just as active. Christabel disrupted a Liberal Party meeting in 1905, demanding votes for women. Sylvia designed posters, banners and badges.

Richard   Emmeline

Go to prison!

'By breaking the law, Mrs Pankhurst and the suffragettes knew that they ran the risk of punishment. And punished they were, over and over again. Each time they took part in a violent protest, they were arrested, put on trial, found guilty, and sent to prison. There they were treated harshly. The British government hoped that this would stop them protesting again.

'Many people admired the suffragettes – I know I did! But others felt that if women behaved like criminals, they could not be trusted as equal citizens – or as voters.'

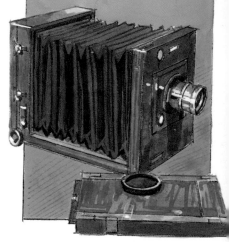

LOOK OUT FOR SPIES! The British police are using some of the world's first long-distance cameras to take secret pictures of suffragette protesters. So wear a big hat or a fashionable veil to hide your face.

Prepare for prison!

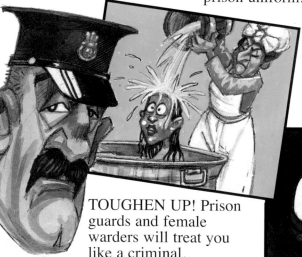

BE BRAVE! You'll be roughly handled when you're arrested.

TOUGHEN UP! Prison guards and female warders will treat you like a criminal.

BRRR! UGH! You'll be searched, bathed and dressed in a scratchy prison uniform.

POOR FOOD. You'll only get bread and water. Chances are you'll fall ill.

LONG NIGHTS. Lights go out at 8.00 p.m. After that you're not allowed to speak until morning.

16

Imprisoned for fighting for my freedom – where's the justice in that?

Handy hint

Make new friends in prison. You'll meet suffragettes young and old from many different places.

WEAR YOUR PIN WITH PRIDE. British campaigner Sylvia Pankhurst designs a brooch that looks like the iron gates of Holloway Prison, where suffragettes are locked up. American protesters wear 'Jailed for Freedom' pins.

Torture and tragedy

'Their violent protests were not working, so the suffragettes decided to try a new tactic. Now, instead of attacking public property, they planned to make victims of themselves. They would risk their lives and health by going on hunger strike in prison! They hoped this would force the government to give in to their demands, rather than see them starve to death.

'Millicent Garrett Fawcett, a wise, experienced campaigner, continued to lead lawful, old-fashioned protests. But these peaceful protests were ignored.'

CAT AND MOUSE
Angered by the suffragettes' tactics, the British government passed a new law. Suffragettes who went on hunger strike were set free until they were strong and healthy again. Then they were arrested and sent back to prison. Suffragettes called this law the 'Cat and Mouse Act'.

DEATH DIVE. In 1913, suffragette Emily Davison ran out in front of the King's horse at the Derby, the most important race of the year. She was knocked down by the horse and died a few days later. A note calling for votes for women was found pinned to her clothes. Was she mad, or a heroine? Or was her death a tragic accident? People could not agree.

THE CAT AND MOUSE ACT
PASSED BY A LIBERAL GOVERNMENT

THE LIBERAL CAT!
ELECTORS VOTE AGAINST HIM!
KEEP THE LIBERAL OUT!

A poster protesting against the 'Cat and Mouse Act'

Handy hint
Keep your spirits up! Dame Ethel Smyth has composed a cheering song for suffragette prisoners to sing.

'Shout, shout, up with your song!'

Keep the blasted woman still, can't you?

PRISON DOCTORS force-fed hunger-strikers by pouring liquid food down a tube and straight into their stomachs. The doctors said this was done to save the protesters' lives. The suffragettes said it was torture.

It's for your own good, love.

No surrender... no surrender...

19

Look west!

Cousin Mabel takes up the story.

'American suffragists were making better progress at this time. We faced a setback in 1875, when the Supreme Court declared that women – although citizens like men – did not have the same rights. But our campaigns finally got results when men began to realise how strong and capable women could be. Way out West, women built homes, ploughed fields, reared livestock and defended new communities. By 1896, Wyoming, Utah, Idaho and Colorado had given votes to women. By 1914, Washington, California, Oregon, Kansas, Arizona, Nevada, Montana and the Alaska Territory had followed suit.'

'THE AWAKENING': This suffragist poster advocated that eastern states should give votes to women – as many western states and territories had already done.

WOMAN POWER. Gradually women got to vote in local elections. Male candidates had to listen to them – and their demands for equal rights.

So – what do you say to that?

Get together!

Cousin Mabel continues.

'When women living in the eastern states saw what their sisters out West had achieved, they were inspired to fight for the vote too. In 1890 the two main suffragist organisations united (see page 12). This gave them renewed strength. In 1913 over 20,000 suffragists marched through the streets of New York City. By 1915 there were 40,000 marchers. By 1917, New York's women finally had the vote.'

HOW LONG MUST WOMEN WAIT FOR LIBERTY?

MR. PRESIDENT WHAT WILL YOU DO FOR WOMEN'S SUFFRAGE?

PICKET LINE. By 1917 many women in the US still had no vote. Suffragists decided to picket the president in the White House in Washington, DC.

SUFFRAGE PARADES in New York and Washington were led by a young woman dressed as the Herald of Liberty, riding an impressive white horse.

Forward into Light!

I'm not mad. I'm furious!

THE PICKETS were imprisoned and went on hunger strike. Picket organiser Alice Paul was put in solitary confinement and the authorities tried to prove she was mad.

Handy hint

Be patriotic! Think of the Statue of Liberty as a suffragist symbol – she's a woman, after all!

TRAGIC HEROINE. The rider on the white horse was Inez Milholland (later Inez Milholland Boissevain), a lawyer and writer. She gave lectures and took part in protests throughout the United States, despite being seriously ill. In 1916 she collapsed from exhaustion and died six weeks later. She was only 30 years old.

INEZ MILHOLLAND BOISSEVAIN

WHO DIED FOR THE FREEDOM OF WOMEN

War effort

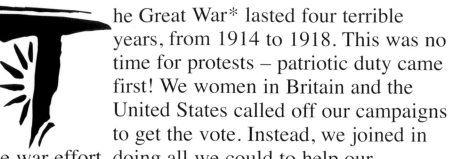

'The Great War* lasted four terrible years, from 1914 to 1918. This was no time for protests – patriotic duty came first! We women in Britain and the United States called off our campaigns to get the vote. Instead, we joined in the war effort, doing all we could to help our countries and our menfolk fighting overseas. We worked as nurses, as women had done in many wars before. But, for the first time, we also took on many jobs that were usually done by men. To everyone's surprise – except ours, of course – we proved that we're strong, hard-working, trustworthy, clever and quick-thinking. Now everyone respected us!'

Who says engineering is harder than sewing?

* *later called the First World War*

Next stop: equality!

WE CAN DO IT!
In wartime, women worked as firefighters, farmhands, engineers, builders, and as drivers and guards on buses, trains and trams.

WOMEN NURSES travelled to the front line, to the thick of the fighting. They showed great courage, caring for soldiers in battlefield hospitals and driving ambulances through gunfire to rescue the wounded.

Whimper!

Hide your grief at seeing so many fine men die. The survivors need you to be strong.

Chin up, old girl!

MILLIONS OF MEN died in the war, leaving their families all alone. War widows had to look for work to pay for food and housing.

YOUNG, EDUCATED WOMEN took over professional men's jobs, becoming doctors, lawyers and professors. Now everyone could see that women are not stupid!

Victory!

Edith

'We worked so hard during the war that our claims could no longer be ignored. In 1918 the British Parliament gave the vote to all British women over 30. This isn't quite equality – men can vote at 21 – but never fear, we're working on that!'

Mabel

'The law has been changed in the United States too. Thanks to the 19th Amendment of 1920, all American women can vote. It's victory! Our long struggle is over!'

Success!

We did it!

Well worth the effort, I say!

DO YOUR DUTY! Vote wisely and you'll be rewarded. From 1928, British women over 21 will get the vote, just like men.

Ballot box

26

Ballot paper

A LIFE IN POLITICS. The right to vote is just one part of women's equality. Now we can also take part in mainstream politics right alongside men. We can hand out leaflets, go on marches, raise funds, sit on committees and run for election as members of Congress or Parliament. We're equal, and we have a lot to say!

Madam Speaker...

What happened next?

Women in Britain and the United States were not alone in campaigning for the vote. Capable, confident women in many countries worldwide also demanded the right to take part in politics. Their success depended on winning support from male politicians and from religious leaders and traditional elders in each nation.

Gradually, a woman's right to vote has spread round the world. Today, it is almost, but not quite, universal. What would Great-Aunt Edith and Cousin Mabel have to say about that?

THIS MAP gives a general idea of when different countries gave women the same voting rights as men.

PIONEER POLITICIANS. There have been many female politicians since women won the vote. India, Sri Lanka, Germany, Israel, the Philippines, Norway, Argentina, Pakistan and many other nations have all had women heads of government or party leaders. Margaret Thatcher (left) was Britain's first woman Prime Minister, from 1979 to 1990. Barbara Jordan (right) was the first African-American woman from a southern state to be elected to the US House of Representatives (from 1973 to 1979).

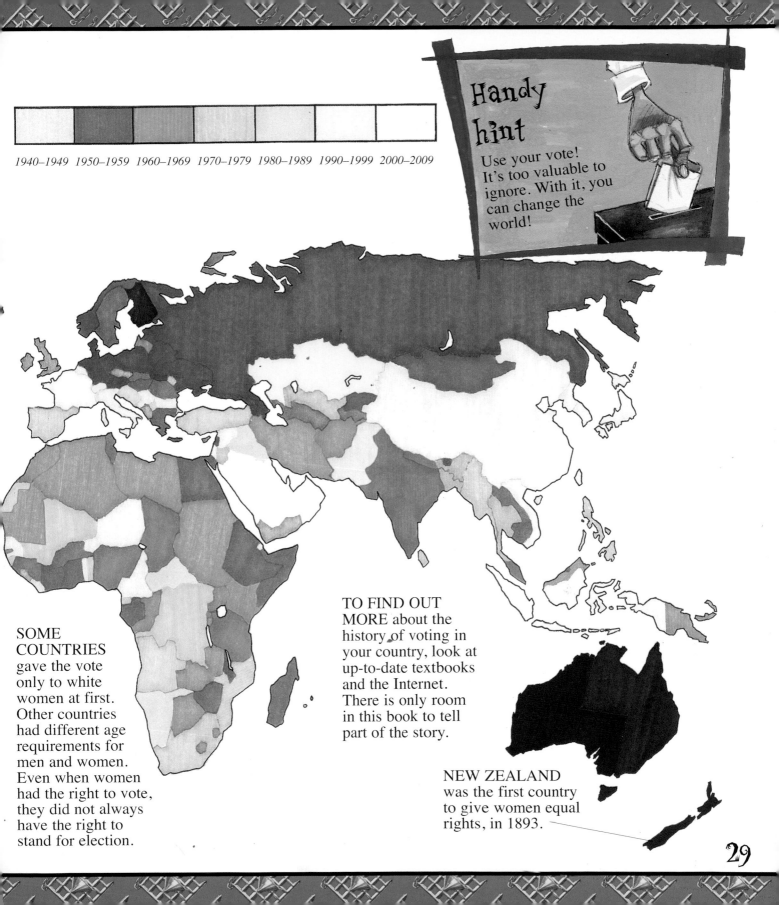

1940–1949 1950–1959 1960–1969 1970–1979 1980–1989 1990–1999 2000–2009

Handy hint

Use your vote! It's too valuable to ignore. With it, you can change the world!

SOME COUNTRIES gave the vote only to white women at first. Other countries had different age requirements for men and women. Even when women had the right to vote, they did not always have the right to stand for election.

TO FIND OUT MORE about the history of voting in your country, look at up-to-date textbooks and the Internet. There is only room in this book to tell part of the story.

NEW ZEALAND was the first country to give women equal rights, in 1893.

29

Glossary

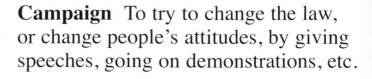

Ballot box An official box in which voters put their ballot papers when they vote. The papers are locked in the box until it is time for them to be counted.

Ballot paper An official form for voting. It has a list of candidates printed on it, and voters make a mark against the name of the candidate they want to elect.

Campaign To try to change the law, or change people's attitudes, by giving speeches, going on demonstrations, etc.

Chartists Members of an English organisation (1838–1848) which demanded new laws, including allowing all English men – not just landowners and men with property – to vote.

Colonist A person who settles in a foreign country but is still loyal to his or her home country.

Committee A group of people who meet together to organise something, such as a political campaign.

Equality Treating people fairly, whatever their sex, age, skin colour, religion, etc.

Great War A name that was often given to the First World War (1914–1918), especially before the beginning of the Second World War (1939–1945).

Hunger strike A form of protest in which the protester refuses to eat or drink until their demands are met.

Liberal In favour of progress and political reform.

Liberal Party A British political party (1859–1988). Until the 1920s it was one of the two main parties in Britain, and was often in government.

Lobby To meet with politicians and try to persuade them to change the law.

Patriotic Supporting one's own country against foreign enemies.

Petition A document signed by a large number of people, demanding a change in the law.

Picket line A line of protesters who try to prevent people from getting into a particular place unless their demands are met.

Quaker A member of the Religious Society of Friends, a Christian group which believes in pacifism (not going to war) and equality.

Solitary confinement A form of imprisonment in which the prisoner is kept alone and not allowed to meet or speak to anyone.

Speaker The chairman or chairwoman of the British House of Commons or the US House of Representatives.

Suffrage The right to vote.

Suffragette The nickname given to British women who campaigned for the right to vote.

Suffragist The name preferred by American women who campaigned for the right to vote; also, a member of the National Union of Women's Suffrage Societies in the UK.

Temperance movement A group of people who campaigned against drunkenness.

Index